CAPSULE
STORIES

Masthead

Natasha Lioe, Founder
Carolina VonKampen, Publisher and Editor in Chief
Claire Taylor, Editor
BEE LB, Reader
Aimee Brooks, Reader
Stephanie Coley, Reader
Rhea Dhanbhoora, Reader
Hannah Fortna, Reader
Teya Hollier, Reader
Mel Lake, Reader
Kendra Nuttall, Reader
Rachel Skelton, Reader
Deanne Sleet, Reader
Annie Powell Stone, Reader
Emily Uduwana, Reader
Amy Wang, Reader

Cover art by Darius Serebrova
Book design by Carolina VonKampen

Paperback ISBN: 978-1-953958-18-1
Ebook ISBN: 978-1-953958-19-8

CAPSULE STORIES

Winter 2022 Edition

Hibernation

Contents

Hibernation

You wake up cold despite the layers of quilts atop your bed. Snuggling closer to your warm partner, who's sound asleep, you remember you don't have to work today. You try to remember what day it actually is. But it doesn't matter. Today, for the first time in weeks, you have nowhere to be but here. Home.

The wind howls against your window as you pull on warm socks to guard against the cold of the kitchen tiles. As you pad down the hallway into the kitchen, your cat weaves between your legs, chasing your warmth. The coffee machine whirs, breaking the calm quiet of the house, and you look out at the freshly fallen snow blanketing the ground in sparkling white. You couldn't go anywhere today even if you wanted to. The roads are covered, and the snow is still falling thickly. A silence has fallen over the street; even the squirrels that usually hustle and bustle around your neighbor's bird feeder are tucked away in their homes this cold winter morning. Everything seems to be saying slow down, there's no need to be productive today. Just rest.

Steaming mug in hand, you burrow into the couch, surrounded by a pile of books you got for the holidays and a brand-new notebook. A tin of fudge from your grandma. A candle that smells like Christmas. A string of lights glowing. A warm blanket your friend knit and your purring cat. All you need to rest and hunker down for the rest of the winter as the cold lingers in these short, dark days.

Sanctum

Maureen Adams

mercury drops
daylight dwindles
winter turns me inward
body and soul

the push to be
out amongst disappears
except when fresh drifts call
to solo snowshoes

batteries recharge
in seclusion
the pace suspends
soups on simmer
roasts done low and slow

read more
travel back with classics
linger over
games and puzzles

dust off projects
that patiently awaited
this season's endurance
plod through piece by piece
as winds howl and dark descends

[december]

Katelyn Grimes

white pine needles
split the difference
between prophecy and promise
while i rest
in a hotel room

i don't know what it is exactly about winter
there's scarf fuzz sometimes
and the opaque window of ice
where i want to paint
forgetting i don't know how to paint

i don't know exactly
how the last repetition
is in conformity with time
"chronological" is precisely the reason
for being tangled up in (in)significant things

the subtle frost (unexpected talisman)
reaches into the far corners of my mind
probing my hippocampus
setting off a series of obscurely connected neurons
one firing after another

to generate a memory
of words on scrap paper
held afloat by
a candle called dark wood
and a song called "dark waltz"

then i'm on a bridge
with an untied shoelace
instead of in the bathtub with six books of poetry
while the wick burns and the record plays
a private dilemma

subtle frost

reaches

into the far

corners

of my mind

[swan song]

Katelyn Grimes

today's forecast called for snow,
a prediction indifferent
to the calendar's early border for spring,
as well as to my own personal feelings on the matter.
winter has these silences,
hidden between the refrains
of wind pushing past pine, through buildings, rattling
windows and bones.
perhaps hypocritically, just this week
i'd considered resurrecting
my christmas music playlist to manufacture a cheeriness
i could not seem to come by naturally.
i expected even this would not shake it;
i've been there before and know
the silences lie in wait,
buried beneath the song that gets stuck in my head
(but only about four lines of it, the only lines
i can independently recall, no matter how many times it's been),
and then the mental voice
(this one sounds more like mine)
rereading the last elusive passage
of the book you recommended
years ago and i'm finally getting to it—
no, it wouldn't do.
what i attempted instead, inviting spring indoors,
also failed; perhaps sensing my infidelity,
my potted plant, the only real
one among artificial succulents and stems,
wilted spectacularly, suffocated

by shadow and scant light from a sun
retreated to relic.
i knew the silences;
i couldn't say it was without warning
when it went cold, withered to ghost,
and i couldn't say
it didn't make me think that
in the end,
maybe we were built to mourn.

winter has these silences
[hidden between the refrains]

[raðljóst]

Katelyn Grimes

a haloed lamppost
interrupts the snow, tethers
all of existence.

Solstice Shivers

Evie Groch

Winter arrives without my welcome,
dropping clues for many weeks.
Like a thief, it's been robbing me of daylight,
stretching evenings out too long.
It fades to dark when I'm still working,
steals my light, makes me close up shop.
It's more stubborn than I can be,
will not bend to my fervent wishes,
leaves no choice but to bend to its.

I turn up the heat, put the pot on the stove,
simmer the stew until it releases
its inviting aroma, what I need to build
stamina for hibernation.
My peasant roots plead
for kasha and bowtie pasta.
I settle down with a tall glass of honeyed tea.
Its amber tone speaks to me,
assures me of my resiliency, calms my
solstice shivers, guarantees I will survive.

I do not knit, crochet, or quilt,
so I sequester myself in writing,
pour my heart out on snowy pages,
shovel them into piles,
settle in to read poems and prose,
sleep deep in lyrical lines.

When daylight breaks, I open the drapes,
discover again what I yearly forget.
The wonderland beyond my window
glistens in white lace, icy stillness,
feathering mounds of soft pillows
awaiting my exhale of delight.

*sleep deep in
lyrical lines*

Unexpecting

Anna Dobbin

My duvet cover is white with a crisscross texture, a grid pattern, an expanse of tiny squares. I pick up the corner and start counting the squares. There are twenty-eight in a row about a foot long.

I search my inbox for the order confirmation email from when I bought the duvet. Click the link, find the duvet, scroll down to the specs. It's nine by seven and a half feet.

I close the browser and open the calculator app. Do the math.

My duvet cover has an estimated 52,920 squares.

If I wanted to confirm my estimate, I could count them one by one. I do some more math. Going at an easy pace of one square per second, it would take about 14.7 hours to count them all.

These days, I have that kind of time.

I count until I fall asleep.

At the fertility clinic, I was feeling a little queasy as I sat on the exam table with a sheet over my bare bottom half. Just nerves, I thought to myself. The nurse walked in wearing a white lab coat. We chatted for a few minutes about what to expect that week: an ultrasound and bloodwork today, Tuesday; a hysterosalpingography on Thursday; a few tests for my husband, who was in the clinic's waiting room. All of this, the nurse explained, was the standard initial workup for couples struggling to get pregnant.

I lay back on the table, and she gave me a brief warning before reaching under the sheet and inserting the ultrasound probe.

Seconds later, looking at the screen, she said, "Well, I guess we can cancel your HSG. That's a baby." She pointed to a dark oval with a light gray dot inside it.

I was speechless for a moment, then blurted, "Holy crap."

"It's measuring at five and a half weeks."

I asked if my husband could come in. The nurse fetched him, inserted the probe again, and let me repeat the news. My husband's eyes filled with tears. I could tell that he was smiling under his mask.

After the exam, as we walked to the car, ultrasound pictures in hand, we alternated between stunned silence and giddy giggling.

On Sunday, nauseous and exhausted, I crawled into bed. Covered myself with my white duvet.

That was two months ago, and I'm still here.

You hear stories about difficult pregnancies. My sister-in-law was ill the entire time she was carrying her first daughter. An acquaintance of mine was recently diagnosed with hyperemesis gravidarum, or severe morning sickness. Another friend is five months along now, well into her second trimester, when she is "supposed" to be feeling better, and she still vomits a few times a week—no anti-nausea medication has worked for her.

But these stories, even detailed accounts of the daily struggle, even vivid descriptions of the physical symptoms and emotional turmoil, can't capture what it actually feels like to lie in bed for two months straight.

The stories can't capture what it's like to eat nothing but saltines and dry pretzels for that long.

What it's like to be unable to stand or walk for longer than ten minutes.

To be unable to do the job that you love.

To be stripped of everything that makes you who you are.

As a society, we have begun to talk a lot about the importance of rest: taking time off work, prioritizing self-care, "listening to your body." But resting when you don't want to rest—forced hibernation—quickly becomes excruciating.

It's the boredom. The isolation. The depression.

I'm doing absolutely nothing, and yet this is the hardest thing I've ever done in my life.

My white duvet rests heavy on my body, like a layer of dense snow.

The bedroom walls are white too. So is the paint on the radiator. My pillows. The window shades. Even my dog, who's stayed faithfully by my side all through these identical days, has mostly white fur. He sheds onto my duvet, but the hairs just blend in.

I begin to wonder why I chose all this white. It seemed classy, classic, before. Now it seems insufferably boring.

My dog burrows under the duvet. He lies down, warm and curled up tight like a cinnamon roll fresh from the oven, with his back against my abdomen.

I spoon my body around his and close my eyes.

When I open them again, two hours have passed.

I listen to an audiobook about pregnancy.

And to think, I used to wish I had more time to nap and to read for pleasure.

I laugh aloud into the empty room.

My dog startles, picks his head up, glances at me with inky eyes.

You know, darkness gets a bad rap.

Defense Against the Dark Arts.

The Dark Tongue of Mordor.

The Dark Side. Darth Vader and Kylo Ren and Palpatine, all dressed in black.

We're supposed to root for the light.

But I don't.

The light hurts my eyes, my head.

And there's nothing that takes the edge off a migraine—a white-hot dagger stabbing my right temple, again and again—like

complete

total

utter

darkness.

For a while, during my teens and most of my twenties, I didn't want children. I was never drawn to babies or toddlers; I didn't possess any kind of natural maternal instinct. Even as a child, on family vacations, I remember trying to hide from my clingy cousin, four years younger than me, to avoid having to play with her. I wanted to hang out with my older brother, not a little kid with a snotty nose.

But if you're a girl, not wanting to have children is a problem. From the beginning of our lives, we're encouraged to be caregivers. Boys are gifted toy trucks and trains; girls are handed baby dolls, some so lifelike that they actually cry and poop and have to be fed.

About two years into my relationship with my now hus-band, we had a conversation about kids. I knew I couldn't marry someone without being on the same page about the existential question of children. I told him I didn't want any. He said he didn't know—he'd never thought about it. To me, this was shocking—that a person in their late twenties had never once considered whether they wanted kids.

But my husband is a man. And men don't go through their entire lives, from the first toys they're given, being told that they should be parents. That their *purpose* is to make babies.

I became aware of my lack of interest in having children—and the fact that this was Not Normal For A Girl—at an early age. It was clear to me that I had to have an ironclad reason for not wanting to be a mom.

I must've been around twelve years old when I started telling people, "I don't want kids because I think childbirth will hurt too much."

Oh, sweetie, it hurts but then it's over. It's worth it!

At age seventeen: "I don't want kids. They're annoying."

There's no greater joy than being a mother!

At age twenty-one: "I don't want kids because I'm too selfish. I want to focus on my own life and do whatever I want."

The love you have for your children is the most profound type of love a person can experience. Having children makes you a better, more selfless person!

At age twenty-four: "I don't want kids because I want to be happy. There's this study that says couples with children are, on average, less happy than child-free couples."

Oh, sweetie, you'll change your mind!

Though my answers shifted over the years, I always had an excuse ready because I thought I needed one. Nobody questions a woman when she says she wants to have kids. "I want children" is a good enough reason to have them.

So why isn't "I don't want children" a good enough reason not to?

When well-meaning boomers told me I would change my mind about kids, I would roll my eyes. Sometimes internally, sometimes literally, depending on my mood.

They happened to be right, in my case.

I have reasons for changing my mind.

But I'm fucking tired of having to explain my reasons.

Well, at least my symptoms aren't so bad that I need to be hospitalized.

At least I can keep bland food and water down. Most of the time.

At least I haven't lost enough weight to worry my doctor.

At least the constant nausea is an indicator that I'm statistically less likely to miscarry.

At least I have a loving and empathetic partner who takes good care of me and whose job supports both of us while I can't work.

At least I'm under thirty-five, not "geriatric" or high-risk.

At least the baby is healthy.

At least I was able to get pregnant at all.

At least, at least.

I keep a circular Tupperware, about the diameter of a dinner plate, on my nightstand. Inside: a mix of saltines, pretzels, sometimes popcorn. My husband calls it my "carb trough."

Every day, I lie on my side, streaming endless hours of TV on my laptop, with the Tupperware open on the mattress next to me. I reach in, bring a snack to my mouth, chew carefully, repeat.

Right now, eating is unpleasant at best. But if I let my stomach get too empty, the nausea worsens. So I eat as diligently as I can.

Until I just can't anymore.

There are days when looking at this goddamn pile of snacks makes me come undone. I blink down at the food and suddenly cannot imagine anything more repulsive. I start ripping at my seams, and I spill out everywhere, and I cannot be contained.

I cry so hard that no sound comes out. Once, I cry so hard that I vomit.

But the thing about these spirals, these cyclones of mourning for the person I used to be, is that they always have a bottom. And when I land there, whimpering, I feel my husband's hand gripping mine, and I finally see him through the smoke and the rubble.

We climb out together.

I gasp until I become still again.

And then, afterward, there's nothing I can do but keep on existing.

So I reach for another pretzel.

Today, I wake entangled in my white duvet. I run my hand across the crisscross texture. I run my hand across my dog's back. I run my hand across my lower stomach, which has started to grow.

The
Waiting
Year

Danielle Weeks

Midnight unlatches:
cinnamon and milk
in a hot cup, the dog
waiting by the door.

The hydrangea head
in the window looks
like a woman unsure
if she's still welcome.

All the green things
have nowhere to go
but down, returning
to the living cradle.

Human Composition

Danielle Weeks

I am cleaning out the dead under-bed boxes
when the neighbor's blue lights switch on,

star the open windows. 4:30 p.m. and dark
on this side of winter, when even the light

is layered for warmth: yellow-glow windows,
a gradient blue-gray sunset, the steady moon

wrapped in white. I ready my gray sweaters
and gloves, close the curtains early, research

the right way to dispose of years-old X-rays:
if they will resist decomposition, if they will

leak into the groundwater, the roots, if a fish
one day will swallow dust from my glowing ribs.

I keep thinking about being eaten, the feast
of the body, a microecosystem in the hollows.

Next year, a person can legally will themselves
back to the soil. After death: the body swaddled

in alfalfa, microbe-warm air breathing them down
layer by layer. The choice of a wild or landscaped

end. I never broke a bone, was never hospitalized
for wildness. But I think I know how close the body

is to nothing, why we string up lights in the darkest
time of year, why I have boxes full of myself stored

under the bed. Here are my papers. Look at these
tax returns and birthday cards, proof of humanity.

Let's pretend I can keep what I earned here,
that I have ordered everything into stillness.

I have ordered everything into stillness

Resolution

Danielle Weeks

I break in the new year with hunger,
blotting a stain from the floor, closing
my curtains against the all-seeing dark.

This is the last hour to make myself
ready for what comes next, to grow
a new coat. The people I know post

pictures of themselves, faces changing
in a grid. I don't let myself remember
the old self, not even the good of her.

But after I clean, I feed her: leftover
soup and bread, sparkling grape juice,
the snow-light space outside myself.

A toast for that girl in her quiet worlds,
the tough braid of her. She didn't know
what she needed, only waited to wake.

Autism in the Wintertime

Izzy Amber Wyskiel

Might I imitate the dove, the owl, the crow
the beings that crest and swoop and sparkle dull
in our white and black skies
in the orbit of our fogged glasses

Might you try it with me, then we can laugh together,
thick-socked boot feet planted in the iced marsh
or the grit of the cold-shocked earth,
      hard as old, forgotten, ruined cake
or the pond transformed to unyielding mirror

Then might we go for coffee?
I'll grab the table while you order for me
I'll shed my layers, drape them on the wooden chair,
itch the places on my skin where disagreeable fabric grated
close my eyes against the needling lights,
the tidal smack of nearby dishes
while I wait for the darkening day
A friend I greet with the low-humming comfort of years invested
and darkest secrets exchanged
with wintergreen breath and fleece-armed embrace
lamplight the color of golden raisin

Winter is when the world is more like me
tired and quiet and craving comfort
Slow activities, slow days, unafraid of shelving energetic displays
or else hungry and wide-eyed for color and celebration
soaking it into the bones, rattling with green, gold, pink, red
fizzy with naive, admirable courage
high on the window view
of the many bright spots
of our fatigued world.

We've Been Waiting

Izzy Amber Wyskiel

time to shed the onion skins, scatter the soap bubbles
of fickle summer naps,
the restlessness of eternal autumn,
and now—slip into the cloak, bathe in the molasses,
lean into the theremin, the thrum, the hum,
the reliable current—of winter daytime slumbers.
snow outside.

crackle-limbed choreography
close the curtains tight, summon rain from a metal box,
turn the volume down, then up,
down a bit, it must be perfect, this soft skewing of reality
chasing sleep, wind at your lips.
snow outside.
birds and squirrels double-lidded,
doubled down, trampled brambles.
the world heals.

surrounded by the still life of your days,
in the cradled cube of your room
things that embarrass you—cereal milk
resting at the bottom of yesterday's bowl, stagnant sweet and pink
things that bring you joy—a stack of still-warm folded laundry
like puff pastry layers, like a cross-section of lovely earth
a crumpled paper
a dust bunny
a love letter
a dozing pet

snow outside—white so bright, it almost strobes
the soft cut of a handful, the sprawl of a land-full
hearty shrubs huddle low,
pines arc in whale-finned angles to a twin sky
turnips like hearts in the ground, squash and cauliflower and
brussels sprouts their confidants
inside, in the hall beside mud-crusted boots,
boxes of string lights sticky with
gray dust, ready for careful attention,
to be lifted high
to adorn white walls, to glow in heavy hope

winter day-
time slumbers

Catnap

Michelle Yim

You and I
Under purl-knit blankets.
Tangled bodies fit together
Each arch and dip of your flesh
Is my own.

Soft tired breaths ruffle baby hairs
From the top of my head.
Each cough
Every quiet snore
Is home.

The curve of your collarbone
The divot at the base of your throat
Your half-moon scar
The scent of fresh laundry.

Into my home
You and I
We sleep when the days turn cold
Guarding each other's warmth.

Frost on Window-panes

Anastasia Arellano

Sandra peers out the curtains, watching the snow fall in thick sheets. Through the frosted windowpanes, headlights flash. Finally. She releases a sigh of relief. The dinner she's been anticipating for the past hour has arrived.

A figure emerges from the car, huddled over, a small lump in their arms. Sandra heads them off, opening the door just as the motion detectors on the front porch illuminate Barb. She freezes in her tracks, caught like a deer in headlights.

"You're letting all the heat out." Sandra waves her girl-friend into their house. "What'd you get for dinner?"

"Actually"—a small meow comes from the inside of her thick coat—"we have a little houseguest."

"No," Sandra whines, taking a step back. "You know I'm allergic."

Barb opens her coat, droplets of snow falling to the carpet, melted by the home's heat. Out pokes a little black face dwarfed by the two ears atop its head. Big, yellow eyes meet Sandra's blue, and she feels a mesmerizing pull as the little kitten begins to purr.

"It looks like a bat." Sandra quickly turns away. She sniffs, waiting for her nose to start running or her eyes to start itching—whatever it is that bodies do when they're allergic.

"Do you want to hold her?" Barb asks in a voice barely above a whisper.

"She is cute," Sandra muses, looking back toward the little black kitten nestled in Barb's arms. "Where'd you find her?"

"She was stuck in a snowbank outside the library. I think someone threw her out."

"She can stay the night." Sandra follows Barb into the kitchen where she gets the little kitten a can of tuna. "We'll call an animal rescue in the morning."

"Poor little thing is starving." Barb continues to feed the kitten bits of tuna by hand, marveling at how voracious her appetite is for such a small cat. "Pour her a bowl of water please?"

Sandra pulls out a shallow ceramic bowl, fighting the smile threatening to spill across her face. Watching Barb nurture such a helpless creature is making her fall in love all over again.

"And just what do you plan on doing when she has to go to the bathroom?" Sandra's stoicism returns the moment she catches Barb's gaze coming toward her.

"I think there's an old litter box and some litter still out in the shed from the previous tenant."

"I trust you to set that up, then?"

Barb nods.

"Good. Preferably the laundry room so it's away from the rest of the house."

Barb nods again. "Sure."

Sandra clears her throat but doesn't say anything more, choosing to return to the living room. She settles onto the couch, turning on the TV as she snuggles beneath her fuzziest blanket. She listens with intent as the meteorologist delivers the forecast, hanging onto his every word.

"And with that, we can expect this storm to last an extra day," the man on TV says with an overenthusiastic glimmer in his eye. "Now back to you, Tom and Cathy!"

As the newscasters begin to discuss the latest celebrity scandal, Sandra tunes out, her eyes drifting to the window once more. Snow has already begun to pile onto the sides of the window, the frost making it impossible to see more than a faint glow of streetlights outside. Two whole days of this. Sandra shrugs. Won't be the worst thing in the world to have to skip another day of work. She and Barb can do a bit of baking together and maybe watch a series or two on Netflix. She smiles at the thought.

"Could be nice to do nothing," she mumbles to herself.

She snuggles into the couch. A tiny yowl from the other side of the couch makes her jump. Sandra peers down to see the little kitten wandering around, crying out.

"What do you want?"

The little kitten makes a beeline for her, tiny tail high in the air like a fluffy toothpick.

"No, no, no!" Sandra protests, but the kitten ignores her, jumping up and settling into the plushness of her blanket.

"Please, no." Sandra's voice lacks all authority as the kitten burrows into the blanket, kneading with such strength for such a small thing. The mighty engine of her purring fills the room.

"You can't stay here," Sandra whispers, watching the adorable display occurring in her lap. "This isn't your home."

The kitten ignores Sandra, contentedly making biscuits until she's overwhelmed by sleep.

"This won't work long term," Sandra says, gently running a finger over the top of her fuzzy head. "I'm allergic."

The kitten curls into her lap, throwing her weight with impressive density despite not possibly weighing more than four pounds. The little engine gradually dies down as she falls asleep.

Sandra sighs. "You're actually quite cute," she admits, watching the kitten's lips and whiskers twitch while dreaming. She sneaks a peek at the tiny fangs.

"I knew she'd grow on you." Barb's voice causes Sandra to jump. Instantly, the roaring engine starts up again, followed by the biscuit factory.

Barb takes a seat on the couch beside Sandra. "So, what name were you thinking?"

Sandra scowls.

"Come on," she says, grinning. "I was watching you two."

"I'm allergic."

"Lies. You're only *allergic* whenever it's something you don't like."

Sandra looks away, unwilling to dignify the truth with a response.

"So?"

"So what?"

Barb's big, pleading eyes bore holes into her heart. "What do you want to call her?"

"Batty. Because she looks like a bat." A small smirk pulls at the corners of Sandra's mouth as she watches Batty tucker herself out once more with her biscuit making.

"Batty Bat." Barb smiles. "I love it."

She leans down and kisses the top of Batty's head.

"And I love you," she concludes, leaving a gentle peck on Sandra's cheek.

Sandra smiles, basking in the glow of her new little family.

"What's for dinner?" she whispers as she strokes a sleeping Batty.

Barb bites her lip, her face scrunching up. "I'm so sorry. I forgot to pick up dinner."

Sandra rolls her eyes but chuckles. "I think there's a pizza in the freezer somewhere."

Barb kisses her cheek once more before going to prepare their dinner. Within fifteen minutes, both women are snuggled on the couch together with Batty, watching a movie. Outside, the snow continues to fall, howling winds echoing in the dark.

"Pizza, you, and Batty." Barb grins. "What more could a girl need?"

"Nothing," Sandra says, reaching for another slice. "This is perfect."

Batty suddenly lunges up, swiping a piece of sausage from the top of her slice. Both Barb and a startled Sandra burst out laughing, their joy carrying through the frosted windowpanes into the wintry night.

Cocooning

Caitlin Gemmell

You light a candle
to remind me
of what is holy.
Voices quieten
as daylight dims
and the candle's glow
hugs the darkness.
You peel the apples
and I chop them,
carefully preserving seeds
to be counted,
fortune known.
In the oven the apples go
with oats, brown sugar,
and cardamom.
We read, silently
together
while we wait
wrapped in a green
velvet blanket.
Winter's kiss drawing us
together
again.

Forecast on a January Evening

Erin Jamieson

My breath catches
as evening paints the sky
ashy gray & dusty rose

Wind pipes down my throat
I can taste snow
that has not yet fallen

Our home looks
so small
it is not difficult to imagine
the roof collapsing
or fragile trees bent
by an ice storm

But you are inside
sipping chai tea
rust & yellow-gold embers
dancing in our hearth

I do not imagine for one minute
you understand the weight
of being on the outside

Promise and Potential, 1881

Valerie Hunter

Peter's son is born in the midst of a blizzard, which necessitates Peter delivering the babe himself since he can't very well fetch a midwife in such weather. It is a strange and terrifying experience, though mercifully quick; Eliza waits to wake him until it's nearly time and gives him brief, whispered instructions. She ends with an admonishment not to wake Lissie, fast asleep in the trundle bed beside them.

Peter didn't know birth could be so quiet, so calm. Of course Eliza's the one doing all the hard work, but he is the one in charge of catching the baby and he has a million questions, none of which he can voice. Even without the worry of waking Lissie, it's not his place to ask, to appear unsure and add to Eliza's anxiety. She huffs and strains, red-faced and sweating, and he does his best to appear calm even when he feels anything but. It is his job as the man of the house to never show his fear.

When he feels himself on the verge of cracking, he steals a glance at Lissie, marveling at the way she can sleep through such an event. Perhaps the frenzy of the storm outside masks their own near silence, but the air in the room still crackles with energy. Still, she sleeps until the baby's cries rise above the sound of the wind, at which point she bolts up and stares disbelievingly at this tiny, red interloper.

Once everything is done, Peter boosts her onto the bed beside Eliza, and Lissie pokes at the baby's fist. Yesterday Lissie's hand seemed impossibly small to Peter, but tonight it is enormous and she looks strangely grown up.

"Your baby brother," Eliza tells her. "Little James."

"Yes," Lissie says, as though she has met James before, and then she promptly falls back to sleep.

Eventually Eliza sleeps, too, the exhaustion easing off her face as she breathes slow and even. The baby has been fed and is wrapped up tight, and Peter is meant to put him in the cradle and return to bed himself, but he doesn't. James is a bundle in his arms that he can't release.

It's the first time he's held a newborn. Lissie was born five months after Peter came out west to stake the claim. Eliza stayed behind with her family in Ohio, hadn't come to join him until Lissie was six months old, already a proper little person who could smile and babble and tug on his nose. Peter was instantly besotted.

Their first son was born the following year, in the waning heat of summer. Peter got the midwife and then made himself scarce, cutting hay till he was soaked through with sweat, keeping an ear out for the sound of the child's entrance. When the midwife finally came to get him, the sun was low and Peter was bone weary. The baby had come and gone while he labored in the fields, and he never got to see him as anything other than a cloth-wrapped bundle, now buried deep in the shade of the cottonwood tree they planted behind the house.

They called him Petey. Eliza suggested calling this baby Petey as well if it was a boy, but Peter refused. He might not be able to give his son a fine tombstone, but he could give him his name for keeps and not make him share it. So Eliza picked James for the new baby, after her pa.

Eliza's father was an intimidating man who never smiled once in Peter's presence. "It's your job to protect her, make a life for her," he told Peter on his wedding day, and those words took root in him.

Peter has tried his best to model himself after this stony, steady man, never voicing his fears or his doubts, doing his best to be a good provider. He's certain he isn't succeeding, but he never voices this to Eliza, too afraid of what she may say.

In truth she's the steady one, so wonderful at doing anything required of her, from birthing a baby to making a home from a little sod cave. She's the one who makes their life, not him. He is a bundle of fear, has been ever since he came out west. He's scared of how much he loves this wild land, scared he'll fail and have to leave it, scared something will happen to Eliza or Lissie, scared for this new baby, especially after tiny Petey, the son he thinks of every day but never knew.

Peter looks down at baby James. He seems to contain all the energy and promise that hummed about the room during the delivery, a tremendous amount for such a tiny body. Do all newborns feel so full of this undefinable potential? He wishes he could ask Eliza, but she's asleep, and anyhow it isn't the type of question he can actually put into words.

He holds the baby close, appreciating the warmth of him. The wind continues to howl, but they're snug and safe inside the soddy, have everything they need. Peter hated his first two prairie winters, being stuck inside with too little to do and too much time to dwell on all his worries. Now he thinks it's not so bad and wishes he could stay in this quiet moment forever. Perhaps this is what winter is for, to make a person realize that life isn't all bustle and work. To give him time to marvel at the tiny miracles.

James stirs slightly and nuzzles Peter's chest. He is aware that this moment won't last and tries to imagine James ten, fifteen, twenty years from now, all that potential blooming forth in a hundred different ways. Suppose that he turns out like his grandfather? The name James conjures that impossible-to-live-up-to man, a terrible thing to saddle a baby with. Not James, then. Little Jim. He whispers the name into that tiny, perfect ear. Little Jim can grow up to be whomever he pleases, can wear his heart on his sleeve and say whatever comes into his head without fear.

Peter smiles down at his son and cradles him closer, trying to absorb just a little of his boundless potential. Tomorrow, he decides, he'll ask Eliza to tell him how Lissie and Petey felt in her arms. He will find the words to ask all his impossible questions, the courage to express everything he feels.

Perhaps this is what winter is for, to make a person realize that life isn't all bustle and work.

Hibernation

Esther Lim Palmer

I heard a black bear
gave birth to her cub
in this cabin.

I felt her wild heart, heavy
with darkness. Clawing
uncertain space.

I wondered why she left
the wild to give life
in this human home.

I longed to know if her cub
had grown. Had gone. Strong
into the wild. To know why
she remained
this way. *Please stay.*

I sat up in bed. Then lay
back down again. Like
a bear in hibernation.
Minutes lost in hours.
Hours like generations.

The End of November

Andrew Calis

Like they must go and are late
the leaves across the street gust, are rushing
east, I think—told like the bones of bears
when it is time, when hibernation

begins.
        The neighbors' wind chimes collide, they are plates
dropped in a sink, and the wind keeps crashing
things into things, one flag tears,
its seams fraying—a sign, the neighbors say,
of some great tribulation.

The season, though, somehow
                                lounges.
                                        It runs late,
the teeth of winter just barely
                                showing,
unseen, still growing somewhere under the earth. Some carry
within their bodies that clock of natural obedience.

How many weeks are left, when the light
outweighs the dark and leaves the sky glowing,
cracks it open? —bluewhite-and-graypinkgold marry,
melt, move; thin, fade in a sudden motion.

Not many, I don't think. All will be right.
Shed the summer skin, quietly hoping
for a quick winter. Sleep. And into windowpane cracks comes air
ice-cold already, and winter like grace slips in.

Something Sturdier than Stone

Andrew Calis

These sudden flakes fall like night, poured
out, glittering from the sky, swept across
the street, scattering like wild children, unmoored
from gravity, wind-shuffled, turning and tossed.
The midday sky is streaked with gray like steel.
Some kids, my kids, prefer to stay indoors
where it is safe. No wind to peel
away the skin with its rough tongue, or roar
through bare trees. No. *Hibernate with me*
while you are small enough to want to stay.
Do you see
how quickly all of this will pass? Today

is backspun, gone, whitened by
the world which spins
like some wild thing. Clouds crash in the sky,
tumble toward each other. In
my ears—the last thing: the past
still calling, the memories of the year before,
the thousand faces we have seen played. Cast
time into stone—into something sturdier
than stone. Place it in my blood, adrift
in veins, a fast-flowing stream, remembered rain-
water rushing like a flood over a cliff,
as deference to memories going on their way.

The Love That Used to Move Me

Andrew Calis

most mornings, love would pull at me, would put
its hands inside my hands and pull me up,
would animate my feet, make air of my smile.

I am older now by many years.
I sit and eat and think. I sleep.
I think I will sleep all winter.

what words are said in the silence
of a look? in the shadow of
movement? leaning on a wall for shape,
leaving only what they were behind—
only breath that spreads through open spaces
like a spill.

Thief River Falls

Abigail Frankfurt

we worked harder in the winter
when the heat was turned off
when there was no gas
when the water went cold
when Cassie's hamster froze
when our laundry became a ball
of ice in the tub we left to thaw
we turned purple to the tips of our fingers
our toes tingled
no heat no heat
and the car wouldn't start
and we loitered in the bars
we went to the deli
used EBT for coffee and fruit pie
sold books and CDs, change for a bus ride
earaches, and empty guts
stole socks from the local shops
groceries from the AIDS project
worked the streets
for what we could sell
the apartment was a shell
all draft and bad temper
pooling our pockets
for the heat we needed
winter went on too long
for slow-circulating ectomorphs
with aggressive appetites
and the radiator shivered
beneath the bluster window
mocking the work we did
snapping twig by twig
slumped on the kitchen floor
in front of the open oven door

Four Walls and Fifteen Heartbeats

Tammy Pieterson

The fumes from that old paraffin heater clung tighter onto our coats than we did onto the holidays. Bedrooms were clogged with luggage, and the wooden floors groaned beneath the extra weight of hand-me-downs and mind games. We met cousins for the first time whose names we couldn't pronounce, with fathers whose faces we would never see. We had so much to share, our stories fell over each other and stretched longer than the icy wind's reach. We drank Milo like water and schemed over the biggest bowl of Grandma's trotter stew. We took short baths, long naps, and a mildly open door was as close as we got to the wrath of outside, hidden from a winter that had already dug into our pores. Like a cave, or a burrow, or a secret—seemingly dead, but itching with life. We were cold, but our hearts were wrapped in the thickest blankets.

Sugar Maple

Erika Seshadri

follow me to the maple forest
dusted in fresh fallen snow
to stillness
to silence
where air bites
the tip of your nose

we'll tap sap
from xylem
in the slow flow of life
one drop at a time

there's no hurry here

this is how
we find sweetness
in the dead of winter

My Father Takes Me for Donuts

Grace McGory

Winter in New Jersey is a bitter ex-lover who never quite goes away. Just as you start to long for her again, she comes back and reminds you why you were so desperate to be rid of her in the first place. She's beautiful and vicious in turns, decorating the world in shimmering, dusty white before biting your cheeks raw and tumbling away. And she loves to remind me she's not leaving anytime soon by taking up residence in my childhood home, making my bedroom the coldest in the house.

My hometown is sleepy in the early mornings. In the summer, there's silvery fog. In the spring, a spectral blanket of pollen. In the winter, there is shimmering snow, early orange sunsets, and my father crusading out into the witching hour.

My father wakes up early and drives for a living. He does not stop for the cold and wind. Some nights, he will leave my mother and me in the living room at six o'clock, and when I am turning in at midnight, he will be shambling out of his bedroom and into the forgiving heat of the shower. And then, he will be gone into the mist of the morning, doing his job before even the sun, traipsing from city to city to be home before I return from school. He says he does this so he can be with my mother and me during the day.

And yet, once a month, he sacrifices his Saturday, one of two days when he can sleep in till a healthy 4 a.m., to do this with me. Today he is not working. These mornings are for us.

Calloused hands brush my hair from my forehead and stir me awake. It's on the near side of five in the morning. Outside, it is winter-dark and my bedroom is a closed treasure chest.

"Come on," says my father. "It's time. Let's go." Even in my perpetual teenage rumple, I was never bothered by the early wake up. I roll out of bed as he beckons me with a smile that I'm told looks like my own.

I'm leaving the house, but it doesn't feel like it. I don't change out of my flannel pajamas, scampering between the house and the car. I am a small mammal trundling through my tunnels of powder, stepping in the larger prints my father makes in the snow before me. When we pull out of the driveway, my father turns the heat on, and the Toyota becomes a moving matchbox, full of warmth. It would be so easy to fall back asleep in the passenger's seat, but I never do.

We pull into the freeway in a comfortable quiet, until my father looks over at me from behind the wheel.

"What've you got for me this time?" he asks me, and I pull up my Spotify and play him the music I've discovered since the last time we did this.

I'm terribly blessed to live so close to New York City. When I was younger, it was all fleeting, unreal magic. As I grew, it became storied. New York is a black-and-white map in my mind with a smattering of colorful pins. The ice cream shop, aptly named Big Gay Ice Cream, where I first told my parents I was queer. The Lunt-Fontanne Theatre, where I stared enraptured at the actors on roller skates and realized, with the jubilance only a child can contain, that that was exactly what I wanted for the rest of my life. Wave Hill Gardens, where my closest friend and I braved the traffic of the Bronx for the first time with a healthy cocktail of fear and laughter.

This place has a special pin on the board. Perhaps it's shaped like a star. Maybe not *You Are Here* but *You Wish You Were*. It's a donut shop on the Lower East Side. The front of house is no bigger than my living room. They make artisan donuts with strange shapes and flavors. We always buy a dozen, and we always eat the same ones first. My dad gets crème brûlée. I get peanut butter and jelly. We bring a coconut crème home for my mom. The others will be picked upon, broken into pieces with our fingers and shared, throughout the coming days. This is our destination.

We pass under bridges and streetlamps with a line of trees on either side of us. Often, we are the only ones on the road. And my father talks. He does not do this usually. We talk all the time, but now, he is *speaking* to me. He is sharing the wisdom of each year when he was my age, giving me the rings of a tree one by one, as if I do not sleep in his childhood bedroom, as if his initials are not carved into the doorframe.

"She never deserved to be your friend," he tells me, and "I think you think people hate you much more than they actually do."

He does not even look at me when he tells me, "All I have ever wanted from you was for you to be kind. And you're so much more than that." I don't need to make eye contact to know he means it. Nobody can hear us. We are warm and alone in the car, and we are our only witnesses, moving along the highway surrounded by the good kind of soft noise. The snow falls and builds itself into walls around us.

"If you don't believe anything else I say, please know that there has never been a father more proud of his daughter," my dad says. I smile out the window. I don't have to respond. He pats my knee.

We drive over the GWB. I take the same picture out the passenger side window that I take every time we do this. The sun is beginning to rise, and the bridge glows with gold light, reflecting off the Hudson. My music is still playing. My dad likes this one. I tell him the title and send the link for the music video to his phone.

He tells me the names of all the buildings we pass, all the hospitals he services while we're still asleep. That one needs more blankets. This one can't decide what color embroidery they want on their coats. That one just signed onto his company. There's not a soul to be seen in any of the windows. Even the city that never sleeps is still hunkered down, buried in blankets and sheets, socked feet yet to touch the cold floors.

When we pull up to the front of the donut shop, my father parallel parks without flinching, a superpower, as I see it. He jumps into the snow piled up against the curb to hold the door open for me. We're the first ones in the store and the only ones in sight on the street.

"Pick what you want," my father instructs. I do, pointing out three or four flavors from the pristine glass case. He does the ordering while I stare at the drink menu, knowing already what I'm getting.

Before I can even voice it, my father tells the front counter lady, "And a hot chocolate for her." He gives me a wink, in a way that's somehow both childish and fatherly in equal measure.

It's my job to hold the box on the way home. The fresh donuts inside leave steamy circles on my pajama pants, absolving me of the shiver I'd picked up between the store and the car. The heat is cranked. The sun is rising. The world is an unshaken snow globe, quiet and still.

And we talk more. It's easier now, lighter. There is nothing outside that we need to consider. Laughter spills into the air and wakes up our cold bones. The sky is a bright blue that I cannot help staring at. A new song is playing, and my father expertly whistles along to it.

We are neither inside nor outside. We're moving, but we're resting. It's early, but we're not tired. Peace is donuts and a bright blue sky and the Hudson, and hot chocolate settling comfortably in the pit of my stomach, just beginning to yawn with hunger.

We return to the house as morning heroes, our bounty in recycled brown boxes, held in hands warmed by to-go cups. My mother is awake, and she greets us at the door. She hugs me in the foyer smelling like coffee, and she kisses my cheek. She does not ask what we talked about, but somehow, I can feel she knows. She kisses my father as I walk up the stairs.

The television is already on, and the show has been queued and paused. By the time my coat is shucked and my boots are on the shoe rack, our donuts have been paper-plated and left at our usual spots on the couch by my dad. My mom takes my feet in her lap as she presses play, and while her eyes are turned away, I share a smile with my father.

The world is this living room, and the world is cozy, and the world is these three people eating donuts and watching true crime and existing together. We are at rest. There is nothing to be done except be *here*. In fact, there is nowhere else to be.

In a month, I will ache with the familiar melancholy of New Year's Eve. I will drink sparkling cider alone on the love seat, from a fancy glass that I will wash right after so I don't leave dishes in the sink. I'll stare at the snow outside, glowing orange from the streetlights, instead of watching the ball drop.

A month after that, my mother will refuse anything for her birthday. When I make her a strawberry shortcake by the light of the oven—because our overhead light has not worked for years—she will cry happy tears, hold my head to her chest and take pictures of the sloppy frosting letters I wrote on top. She won't eat a slice until I have one too.

And my dad won't ask me what school's like, how my friends are, if there's anything I need to talk about. It seems sometimes that he can't, outside the put-away space of his car on the highway at five in the morning.

He'll say it in other ways, though. He'll ask me to play
Resident Evil with him, which really means he'll watch me play
from the couch while teaching me the tricks he learned when
he first played it years ago. He'll ask me the name of that song
I played for him, and days later, I'll hear him plucking out the
notes on the guitar he brought out from storage. He'll turn
his tablet toward me while on a work call to show me a video
of a cat, trying to hide the sound of his smile over the phone.

Right now, though, we're not leaving. Right now, there's
warmth, and a Netflix show we're not watching, and flaky
sugar on our fingers. Coconut crème, peanut butter and jelly,
crème brûlée, side by side by side. We are here for the winter.
We need not leave. Home is here. And in these frozen days,
home has some damn good donuts.

There is nothing to be done except be *here*.

Winter's Sweet Solace

Ginger Dehlinger

Give me the hush
of a pillowed January morning,
snug as a fur-robed ermine
in its muffled den.

With another Christmas stored
in photographs
cookies in the freezer
boxes in the attic
and an extra pound or two on me,
December's pressures
melt from my shoulders
like butter in hot buttered rum.

Cocooned in fleece,
I sink into my tufted mushroom chair
with a mug of hot chocolate
and a book I won't finish till spring.

Picking a Christmas Tree

Lotte van der Krol

Every year I await them eagerly. I watch the little square in front of the old library, flanked by the new mall and the McDonald's, for signs of greenery and a chain-link fence, never sure exactly when they will show up. Until one morning, as if grown up from the cobblestones overnight, the Christmas trees appear.

My mom and I lock our bikes and approach the fence to begin our yearly tradition of picking a tree. The fresh scent of pine greets us, reminding me of long summer days in the forest, winter days in the warmth of home as the world freezes outside. The scent has to fight against the car exhaust and the sugary smell of fried dough from the oliebollen stand, but as we come closer it's almost strong enough for me to imagine myself in a real forest.

We've been buying our Christmas trees from this family of sellers since I was a small child. Back then, their little pop-up tree market was located in the middle of the old town center, sprawling over the wide stone bridge between the canals. It grows smaller every year. Most people nowadays go to the garden center where the trees are picture perfect, exactly Christmas green, straight, spotless, and boring.

These trees are different. Home-grown by the sellers, they're all unique. Some have slightly crooked trunks that give them character, sometimes their tops are split in two, their branches are full of dark green needles, and even real pine cones if you're lucky. Brown leaves from their forest home still stick to their needles, their smell earthy and fresh like rainwater. If I squint, I can imagine moss on the street stones, the paper cups and other litter to be fallen leaves, the city pigeons their wood-brethren.

We walk around and scout out this year's options. We live in an old house with high ceilings, so we only look at those that are almost twice as tall as me. One by one, we take turns holding them up by the trunk with our gloved hands for the other to inspect. There are certain things we look for besides height, like a trunk that isn't too crooked, or brown spots on only one side. The branches cannot be too thick and dense or the decorations will not fit, but not so thin you can look right through them. And, most importantly, it needs to be fresh.

A few years ago, one of the sellers showed us that if you pull at the tips of the branches and the needles don't come off, it means the tree has been cut very recently and will last you a good while. By this method we've picked trees that didn't start to fall out till the end of January, even in the warm living room. And having the tree around during the dreariest of months makes such a difference.

December may be the darkest month, but around here, with the sea and its climate always within reach, not the coldest. Only after the New Year has been welcomed by sparks of colorful fire does the real cold set in. Wet cold that creeps through the windows and seeps into your bones. Though to me that is not the worst about January. It's when the sky is blocked by white and gray clouds, for days on end. With the sky gray, the city gray, the light barely shifting till nightfall, I lose my sense of time, place, reality. Only at night is there any color, when the lights that decorate the houses finally turn on, twinkling in the dark.

It's not custom around here to keep your Christmas decorations up till the first signs of spring, but we always try to hold on as long as we can. There's nothing more comforting to me on a dreary January morning than to come down and turn on the glittering beauty of the light of a Christmas tree to fend off the gray darkness. Soft and comforting, like a warm blanket, to protect myself against the cold of the outside world. A reminder of better days to come.

After a long time comparing and debating, we've narrowed it down to one tree. My mom holds it up for me to give it one more thorough look. It's tall enough and only slightly crooked. The branches are nice and full but with enough space for lights and glittering things, and in between the green I spot the real prize: pine cones!

I imagine it in the corner of the living room, shining in the dark of the house, out through the window and into the gray world of a northern winter. A piece of the wild woods inside our home, hunkering down with us till spring, reminding us what is out there to return to when the first snowdrops reappear. Glittering in fake candlelights and colorful glass, so we do not forget the sun.

With practiced ease the tree seller lifts the tree up and through the contraption that squeezes it into a white net. Once it's wrapped up, he hoists it onto one of our bikes, the heaviest part of the trunk on the saddle and the top reaching far over the handlebars. We strap it tightly so it will stay put during the journey back. A touch to his hat and the tree seller is off again, approaching a different customer squinting up at the rows of trees still leaning against the gray chain-link fence.

We take our bikes with a sense of satisfaction, that once again we've managed to find the best tree possible. Then we slowly walk through the hurried city traffic, past people smiling at the ten-foot Christmas tree on a bike, and make our way back home.

In Winter, the Trees

Lesley Sieger-Walls

Quivering, feathered limbs
cast up a murmuration.

Tree branches, now bare,
spider across the gray sky,
weaving and webbing upward.

Trunks may serve as charnels
for walnut shells,
the shade of a bird,
caps of acorns,
and desiccated leaves.

But inside, trees remain rivers,
flowing witnesses to winter.

They are most alive now:
still and waiting,
a resting awareness,
with tangled limbs
rooted in the sky.

if winter was a berry

K. S. Baron

buried in the garden, i'd bloom to holly
when the cold rolled around, grown
from leaf-rot and tree-decay / the snow
echoes against birch bark, blankets
the earth's bed, lays rose roots to rest—

i am the winter's canopy as much as i am
the autumn's mushrooms, moss covered
and nestled under stone / the dormancy
brings a peace most welcomed by bears
and bees, huddling for warmth in the nests—

i roll through soil when the first frost settles,
daffodils lying beneath the woods as they wait
for the familiar face of the sun to return / the holly
thrives at the turn of the seasons when flowers
die back in the woods i wander through.

the canopy is home to me and the squirrels

K. S. Baron

together we embrace the season's chill,
frozen bark on branches and snow glistening
from the limbs / when they jump, i follow
flying into the winter wind with nothing
but the squirrels to carry me through the trees—
the frost's warm hold brings life to a time of year
when the sun sleeps early / the moon wakes
to light up the earth, glistening decay
in the fields and pastures that lie sleeping
under the branches and trees we lurk in.

Small Wanderings

Russell Thorburn

Our fox who has graced us with his hunger,
whose instinct blooms among
the shadowy logs, selects food he can
hunt by his small black nose.
My wife with her burning black hair
leans through the opened window;
if she could she'd escape with him over
the fallen trees, the logs that
small animals use as highways.
Her fingers snap for his attention
where she has thrown sausage;
she wants to follow him to his den
dug out of soft, sandy soil.
Down into the warmth of the earth,
she will dream of a long hibernation.
Not as lost animals but ones
who survive a frost that can never
be kind when green tendrils
stand up to shout their silent death.
She wants to mother the fox
who offers his generous face of red fur.
An intelligence she observes
in his keen nose searching for fresh
morsels; a flicked tail of royalty
when it's time to run again
after staying too long under my wife's
hive of honeyed words. It is that red
fox face that knows more than
other animals within sight of people.

If you are lucky, the fox will reveal
through his gaze the soul's hidden places,
and you will take his broken trails
of the woods with you where you trespass,
an uneasy feeling when quick feet
barely grace the newly fallen snow.

dream of a long
hibernation

Hibernaculum

Frank William Finney

The party ended
during breeding season.

Car doors slammed.
The music stopped.

Quiet fell
around the lake.

Just when the mood
came over us,

the leaves turned yellow,
crimson, brown.

The woods stood
naked, shivering.

Each day our words
grew frostier.

Our breath
rolled rude and visible.

Our fingers
poked like icicles.

Our hearts
turned cold as snow.

What we were
cooled all the heat

as we slid between
the frozen sheets

and growled all winter
in our sleep.

what we were
cooled all the heat

Winter Song

William Reichard

The snow won't stop falling.
It seems like it's been falling

for days. The house becomes
an echo chamber of my fears

and the million different ways
I annoy you and you annoy me.

But isn't it pretty the way the wind
sculpts the snow in rippling

patterns against the fence?
And isn't it lovely the way

the branches hang low
with their heavy white burden?

We piece a life together.
We patch what we can.

All of the windows are intricately
etched by frost. We can't see outside,

exactly, but the sunlight still penetrates.
Isn't it nice that we can stay here,

holed up like bears in a cave?
The drifts grow deeper and

the furnace sings its burning song.
All winter, we sleep under

heavy quilts, yet our ears hear
the snow as it sings in its silence.

*our ears hear the
snow as it sings
in its silence*

we would happen in the winter

Jillane Buryn

If I could rewrite us, we would happen in winter.

In our winter, the one we'll never have, I drive the snow-flooded roads to reach you. The newscaster on the radio warns against unnecessary driving, and my car is tiny, impractical. Dangerous. I skid to a stop along the curb by your house, heart pounding. You watch through your bay windows. With risks like this, neither one of us can ignore how badly I want this. To ask me to come here, you have to want this badly, too.

This July was mind-numbing, hazy. Neither one of us had to think about what we were doing. Did you think about what we were doing? I hope you didn't. I would love to blame the blistering heat instead of you.

Since neither one of us can pretend I came here for any other reason, I don't wait until the end of the second movie to kiss you. There is no second movie. Not here. This is the only part where I let the winter speed us up: not to rush, no, but to maximize the amount of time spent in each other's body heat. It must be difficult, expensive to heat this old house, so we sit side-by-side on your three-seater couch under the only throw blanket in sight. I shiver—no, you shiver, you run colder than me, remember? Our hands touch. I've been noticing your hands for months—this is true in all our seasons. In this one, though, I think better than to tell you. I keep this confession sheltered from my impulses.

In the summer, we were sweaty and impatient. You didn't kiss me for long before we were going upstairs to your high ceilings and noisy air-conditioning unit. Despite my denial, I wore my favorite pair of mesh underwear. You suggested we undress ourselves as soon as we got into the room. You never touched them.

But the winter air bites at me and slows me down and so I straddle you on the couch, keeping you still below me. I let out an involuntary breath when your icy fingertips brush my stomach under my shirt. You try to pull away, but I like a cold touch on warm skin and so I press your long fingers to me, savoring the sting.

The move to your bed is languid. You pin me against your kitchen island on the way, never losing contact, guiding me up the stairs. I want your hands, gorgeous and long, on me as much as possible, sliding under the edges of each layer of clothing. You savor my textures: wool sweater, denim pants, mesh underwear, leaving a trail behind us until there is only skin.

You surprised me. I've never been so intimately present with someone like I was with you and I didn't mean to do it. I melted into you. But you were lying to me, even then. The truth has burned the sense of safety I felt with you. But I did feel it. Maybe that's why I'm rewriting us. To give us a chance in fresher air.

Because I can never be careless in the winter. The cold demands to be acknowledged, and if I do not heed the warning, it will manifest in angry scales along my cheeks and nose. I like myself best when I am both bold and careful, and I am honest enough to bring my own travel-sized makeup remover, night cream, and toothbrush with me on our first night. Face clean and moisturized, two layers applied around my kiss-swollen mouth, I come back to your bed. You smile as your fingers dance across the softness of my cheek.

That first night this summer, after I removed my mascara with whatever I could find in your bathroom, you shepherded us immediately to sleep. You asked me to stay over, but you wouldn't hold me, even with the air-conditioner pointed directly at us. I was too warm, you said. And I apologized. I couldn't sleep at all. Did you notice?

In this snow globe I've created for us, you ask me to stay because you want to hold me. I stay because I carry enough warmth for the both of us. You relax as you envelop my radiating heat in your embrace. We laugh when my feet, the only chilled part of me, trace icy trails up your legs, and together we become a cozy cocoon. Two people drift off in one tangle of limbs. And even as we jostle apart through the night, you reach for me instinctively.

When the late-morning dawn crawls through your windows, you do not rush out of bed to shower. The crisp clouds of breath between us beg us to treasure this because we know our time is limited. I trace your body in small kisses, memorizing the unexpected dip of your waist and the catch of your breath when I find a sensitive section of skin.

Before I leave, we share not one but two cups of coffee in companionable silence. I'm afraid to drive, to go, because the roads are treacherous and what if this is all there is? But you say Wednesday, maybe sooner, but definitely Wednesday. And so I'll come back on Wednesday, until there's no more time left for us. When we say our final goodbye, we decide to leave us here, hidden in the sixteen hours of daily darkness. This is important, we agree, and so we cannot drag us into seasons where we don't belong. We are intentional enough to be honest with each other. Sacred, precious, temporary. By every afternoon after every night we spend together, the snowfall will erase any trace that I was there.

Do not misunderstand me; I am not writing us into winter because I think we would have lasted longer or been something else to each other. I am simply saying: I wish you had taken the time to treat me better. I wish I had taken the time to ask that of you. So, I surrender us to the slowness of winter. May it afford us kindnesses we never gave to each other.

Pausing

Veronica Nation

Winter gets in through a crack in the window
we can't figure out how to patch.
The screens are old
but too expensive to replace, so we stuff
a towel against the sill and shiver into each other.

In these quiet months, we lie dormant,
secluded in silence, exercising caution.
We talk with surgical precision,
careful not to stir the hurt we have nursed.
It's been this way for months––this familiar cold.

And this is how we forgive each other––
in a silence that matches our breathing,
in an appreciation of the thawing that is to come.

Cold House

Michael Colonnese

The woodstove can't keep
up. Only a little
halo around the firebox
is truly warm. No
insulation in the walls,
and the windows, fogged
with condensation from my kettle,
drip down the rotting
sills. I'm wrapped in blankets.
Hooded like some stranger
with a scythe, I hover
by the stove and sip
Red Zinger. Occasionally,
I poke the embers with a stick.
Along the road, the power
lines grow crystalline
with ice. I haven't tried to start
my pickup truck all
week. I'm burning pine slabs—
bark and rot. The last
oak quarter rounds my pile holds
I'll hoard till nightfall.
Earlier, I burned my poems.
A sodden Sunday, late December.

The Stillness and the Change

Claire Doll

Light pulls me out of my dreams, slowly, the way winter thaws to spring. I don't realize I am awake until I see a trail of daybreak dappled against my wall. For a moment, it looks like an oil painting of the rising sun, golden and delicately formed, and then I notice how morning light is different from all other light. It is newer, fresh and untouched. The world is silent, so still that it seems like night, but it's dawn. I am sure of it.

My body is cold, limbs tight and frozen, and I remember through the haze of dreams that it snowed last night. My eyes slowly move toward the frosted window as I peel the curtains away, still lying in bed. Then, I stare. The sky is changing, a canvas of golds and pinks and deep violets. And beneath it, the snow is still, a startling contrast. Beautiful and sparkling and crystalline, quietly existing, like there was never a moment it wasn't there.

I wish it could all stay like this. That dawn would never fade to day, that snow would never melt to spring. But my heart also longs for the warm, lush air that sinks into my skin, for the blue skies and summer sunlight. Every snowflake, every frost-painted surface is artwork, but so are the scarlet leaves of autumn, the bright petals of May. The world splits into many worlds, fractals of warmth and cold and day and night, and I can't decide which one I love most.

But then I remember that it is dawn, that the sky is golden, if only for moments more. The silence is a harmony weaving between trees, pirouetting in the air, and it is the most beautiful sound. As I reach out to touch the window, my fingertips become paintbrushes, carving shapes and lines onto the frosted glass. The world lies still before me, and I realize that it has always been still. That when painted in one blinding, luminescent color, the silhouettes of the tree branches and the sparkling aura of snow rest peacefully, whether I'm awake to see them or not. That it might not look this way ever again. That maybe it is okay to wait, to lie here and watch the stillness and the change, for as long as I can.

I wish

that   snow   would
never melt to spring

A Lingering Languor

Baylee Pawsey

The steam rose
from the coffee mug
tufting in and out
of existence

One of those
February days when
the heat just
can't keep up

and the effort required
to leave the warm cocoon
of bedsheets
was Herculean

Crawling back in and
burrowing into the blankets and
mentally adding to the growing
list of things to do, I

feel a weariness that caffeine
cannot touch
Maybe I can post that mail tomorrow
Maybe I don't have to clean the floor

Maybe I'll just
stay in bed
an hour
(day
week
month)
more

Return of 200 Rotations

Kat Smith

I Thank the longest night, shortest day
the wax of dark
shifts opening room to new light
new sun
new hope in cold quiet days
   I'm growing warmer to

How long do movements take?
the slow steady dance
pliés in sky
   stretched through six months' time
moments caught in the minutes of days
in carved time for luminary dreams
   I too will rest these open eyes

Burrowed in the nest of still dark
hollows to wonder
parts of the whole
the wheel finding its familiar rhythms
pulled by new wind
   dust stirred

Curtains drawn
paper peeled back
look to see what's been painted of the past
   see, time stamps gone
   see, bounty
     in all the futures we may hold

Fruits seeded
        in the minutes of these days
lain in damp soils
wishes on a star
I Thank you
        longest night, shortest day

moments
caught

in the
minutes
of days

In Velvet

Jenny Dunbar

She looked out at the frozen road, a blackest brown loam. Dark as the velvet jacket waiting in her closet all these years, a bespoke vintage item bought from a Soho tailor. Those times had passed, the bad memories of loss and deceit banished. This season, she would celebrate the dark, indulge in its solitude, wrapped in the musky layers of the years through which she had hesitated, or resisted an urge, to be embraced. Each time she had glanced at her jacket in the back of her closet between a yellow shirt and a tweed gilet, she had a nagging feeling of regret, an uncomfortable idea of herself, a too hot season, lack of intention. Now she gently released the garment from its dark niche, felt its unexpected warmth as she slipped into its arms. This season's rhythm haunted her with a new urgency; she sought solace, away from the acid chime of winter.

From the inside, bolstered against the chill, amid a bounty of cushions, each with its degree of weight and comfort, she stared out at the loam, set hard and indistinct against accumulating fog, the road heading to town softly disappearing. She imagined herself disappearing along it out of necessity, if the lines went down, or the post had to be collected, when something else failed. She would brave the outside armed in her jacket of velvet as winter blitzed, scavenging her cheeks, slowly pressing cold into her bones. The secret mantra she carried in her head—*to be, to be, to be*—protecting her as she disarmed winter with each booted step.

Warm coffee on her lips reminded her of the safety of long ago, in the beginning, before carefree simplicity became obsolete and anonymity part of her choice. Acknowledgement of aloneness. There was always a remnant of that self-destruction chasing her, a fragment of the perfect storm that refused to let go. She had worked so hard at acceptance of loss. One day the demons dispersed, and the fragment of the storm was easier to dismiss.

This house had strong walls; its corners bore no grudge, and neither did its rooms contain malice. The windows remained neutral, all seeing. She kept her solitary purpose as the color of the days grew dense with absence of shadow. Just the flickering darkness pervaded. If she pressed her face onto the glass at night, the flickers became snow crystals, their perspective a disorientating mass of chaotic, dancing pins, while her breath made circles on the windowpane.

She shut the noise of time out, burying it inside the sensuality of dreams. Waking fleetingly, she stretched her limbs in contentment under warm blankets. And so she spun, oblivious to an outside of ache or pain, the waiting in the cold. She turned over in her sleep as a dog barked and the days ran by.

The visitors arrived quietly, travelers from afar, carrying stories of long ago, eccentric encounters, banal and profound, so often funny. She embraced their freedom and generosity of spirit.

One had bought linen cloth in many shades of ocher just for the pleasure of its rare earth pigments, texture and weave, and had sailed home with it on the mail boat.

Another brought memories of dancing in the deep south to the rhythm of summer and flamenco.

Songs full of duende and grief.

Notes and anecdotes in juxtaposition with one another wrapped her tightly in their random significance as she dreamed on.

She heard one song, again and again, deep in the folds of memory, when remembering was a tongue touch swaying, long ago at the beginning.

my lover, the liquid night
lays me down
spills desire's
rich sweet,
time
falters

From the easy elegance of deep window seats, she watched the crows peck at the dormant earth as the thaw began. She luxuriated inside the comfort of her velvet jacket. As she stepped outside in it, the tension in her limbs dispersed, and the potent perfume of new earth penetrated her nostrils. The loam wept dewy trails of moisture, softening the ground underfoot. Each day lengthened imperceptibly until the transition was complete, the edges smoothed and viable. The road no longer disappeared into denseness and instead opened and widened out in front of her.

Returning to the house one day, she automatically and quietly undid the jacket and placed it on a hook. Her hands stroked its still warm form, redolent of all she had dreamed and was now becoming.

The lack of intention she had once felt, a hesitation to think better of herself, a sense of sour regret were no longer present. The feelings had melted into a memory, lost in another season. The last clear light of winter shot through the painted glass, catching the velvet jacket inside its strands. She stood and smiled in the space that had offered safety and now sent her certainty.

February,
A Honeyed
Existence

Therese Gleason

Oh, to hibernate
like an animal in a cave,
to curl nose to tail,
snout burrowing soft fur
in humid darkness, lulled
by water dripping on stone,
belly full of food
and fat cushioning bone,
temperature dropping,
heart rate slowing,
thickening viscous blood.

To sleep all day—
all week, all month—
to lie in a nest of fleece
lights out, blinds drawn
doors closed against
the frigid slog,
the relentless gray,
the raw world,
prayers for spring
projected in color
onto a clean white screen unfurled
behind heavy-lidded eyes:
a devotional in cerulean,
gold, and green.

Nor'easter

Therese Gleason

Their backs are turned, the boy in a black jacket
and the girl in a pink parka with a furred hood.

One mittened, one gloved, both with chestnut hair
and snow clinging to clunky boots. The streetlamps

have come on in the gloam, hazy orbs glowing
among the bare limbs of maples, elms, and oaks.

It's midday but it could be dusk or dawn, hard to tell
in the near whiteout—and I remember *Little House*

on the Prairie, how Pa strung a rope between the barn
and the house so no one would get lost in the blizzard.

My children stride through shin-deep flakes
across a smooth white slate. The surface they tread

is not solid ground but the pond, hard and slick
under a blanket of snow, a month of arctic nights

having frozen water and earth: although it's late
February, three Christmas angels remain staked

in the front yard's unyielding dirt. Hanging back,
I watch these twins of mine take their first steps,

walking on water. See how the girl leads the way,
how the wind tousles the boy's hair. *I'm right here,*

I want to say. The stubborn bulrushes poke through snow
at the water's edge, broken but not dead. *What happened*

to the geese? I want to ask. *Where are the ducklings?*
They pick up speed, the distance between us grows,

and I want to shout, *Wait, stop.* I want to freeze
time. The cold steals my breath as my children press on,

throw themselves into a snowbank on the other side,
laughing and breathless. I feel the invisible tether

between us stretching, straining. Snow keeps falling,
like molted feathers shed in downy white drift.

I stride faster to catch up, stumbling. Icy
glitter stings my eyes. They lie back, spreading

their arms to make wings. I hurry to reach them before
they fly away. Breathless, I promise hot chocolate

with marshmallows to lure them back to the nest.
We walk home together, arms linked, three abreast,

their bright voices thawing the numbness in my chest.

thawing the numbness in my chest

April Snow

Therese Gleason

The birds chortle at sunset
despite the heavy sky

clouds pregnant with snow.
This winter won't let go,

reaching into late April with chill
fingers. It feels like January

but for the bright chirping
I can hear but not see

in shadowy bushes and trees,
beady eyes glittering

like dark jewels at twilight,
feathers sighing as the fine-boned

creatures settle into night roosts
on sparsely budded branches.

This is for the nest
crowning the porch eave,

the newborn petals and leaves
resurrecting a dead landscape.

For the morning, a robin
that pecks at frozen ground, unfazed

burnt umber breast glowing
against the white glaze,

tiny engine in his chest
generating its own heat

busy with the work
of staying alive.

*busy with
the work of
staying alive*

Contributors

Maureen Adams is a retired public-school teacher who has lived her whole life in the upper Midwest. She has gratitude for family, friends, and health insurance. She spends her leisure time gardening, hiking, and working to tell small stories of life and death and many points in between. Her poems have appeared in *Trouvaille Review* and *Creative Wisconsin Magazine*, and she was a prize winner in the 2022 Muse Prize through Wisconsin Fellowship of Poets.

Anastasia Arellano is originally from California but now lives in Dublin, Ireland, as a freelance writer. She is a graduate of Trinity College Dublin and holds a master's in creative writing. She's had short stories published in *The Honest Ulsterman*, *Honey & Lime*, *The Hellebore*, *Anti-Heroin Chic*, *Dragon Soul Press*, and *DarkWinter Lit Magazine*, as well as some poetry published in *Smithereens Press*. She recently completed her first solo YA novel, which is now making the querying rounds. When she's not writing, she's cooking, plastering her bedroom walls in storyboards, or seeking inspiration from the Irish landscape. You can follow her on Instagram at @writeranastasia26 and Twitter at @aarellanowriter.

K. S. Baron (she/her) is a freelance writer, a poetry editor at *Last Leaves Magazine*, and a budding digital artist. She loves the nitty gritty of editing—a misplaced comma here, a misspelled name there. Her work has previously appeared in *Spire Light*, *Havik*, *Burnt Pine Magazine*, and others. She has a soft spot for sharp things (like cats and cacti) and always finds herself drawn to the moon.

Jillane Buryn (she/they) is a queer Gemini writer from unceded Lheidli T'enneh territory in so-called Canada, currently based in Venice, Italy. Their interests include tarot, astrology, translation, taking pictures of the sunset, and reading the same books as their friends.

Andrew Calis is a Palestinian American poet, teacher, and father. His work has been published in *America*, *Dappled Things*, *St. Katherine Review*, *Presence*, and elsewhere. He teaches at Archbishop Spalding High School in Maryland. True hibernation is dear to him, but he will settle for what Frost called "just some human sleep."

Michael Colonnese is the author of a hard-boiled detective novel, *Sex and Death, I Suppose*, and two poetry collections, *Temporary Agency* and *Double Feature*. He lives in the Blue Ridge Mountains, near Hendersonville, North Carolina.

Ginger Dehlinger writes in multiple genres. She has self-published two novels (*Brute Heart*, *Never Done*) and a children's book (*The Goose Girl's New Ribbon*). Her poetry has appeared in over two dozen journals and anthologies, and her short story "Francine" was first runner-up in the 2022 *Saturday Evening Post*'s Great American Fiction Contest.

Anna Dobbin is an author and freelance copy editor, proofreader, and conscious language specialist. Her writing has appeared in the middle grade anthologies *The Hero Next Door* and *Totally Middle School*. When she isn't writing, she copyedits middle grade and young adult books, as well as fiction and nonfiction for adults, graphic novels, cookbooks, and more.

Claire Doll studies English education and creative writing at Mount St. Mary's University in Emmitsburg, Maryland. She is editor of her school's literary magazine, *Lighted Corners*, and her short fiction and poetry have won several awards.

Jenny Dunbar is a published writer of poetry based in the UK. She has work included in several literary journals and anthologies, including *Superpresent* and *Vine Leaves Press*. Her novel, *Sweet Earth*, was published in 2014, followed by an anthology, *Thoughts of Time*, in 2016. She writes each day, always fascinated by landscapes of all kinds and the juxtapositions of life. At present, she is working on a collection of very short stories.

Frank William Finney is the author of *The Folding of the Wings* (Finishing Line Press, 2022). His work has been featured in *Livina Press*, *Pocket Fiction*, *Quibble.Lit*, *Taint Taint Taint*, and elsewhere. Born and raised in Massachusetts, he taught at Thammasat University in Thailand from 1995 until 2020.

Abigail Frankfurt is a writer and artist from New York. Her poetry has been published in *LIT Magazine*, *Unbroken* literary journal, *New York Quarterly*, *The Yale Review*, *Dead Skunk*, and Three Room Press.

Caitlin Gemmell (she/her) is a poet and witch living in a woodland in Upstate New York. Her poetry has been featured in *Rue Scribe*, *One Sentence Poems*, and *the minison zine* and is forthcoming in an anthology by *Querencia Press*.

Therese Gleason is author of two chapbooks: *Libation* (co-winner, South Carolina Poetry Initiative Chapbook Competition) and *Matrilineal* (honorable mention, 2022 Jean Pedrick Chapbook Prize). Recent work appears in *32 Poems*, *Indiana Review*, *New Ohio Review*, *Painted Bride Quarterly*, *Rattle*, and elsewhere. Originally from Louisville, Kentucky, Therese lives in Worcester, Massachusetts, with her family. She teaches literacy and works as a dyslexia therapist. Find her at theresegleason.com.

Katelyn Grimes (she/her) studied English and creative writing, psychology, and history at Carthage College. She now lives in Chicago, where she works for an immigration law firm while continuing to write fiction and poetry.

Evie Groch, EdD, is a field supervisor/mentor for new administrators in graduate schools of education. Her opinion pieces, humor, poems, short stories, recipes, word challenges, and other articles have been widely published in the *New York Times*, the *San Francisco Chronicle*, the *Contra Costa Times*, *The Journal*, *Games Magazine*, and many online venues. Many of her poems are in published anthologies. Her short stories, poems, and memoir pieces have won her recognition and awards. Her travelogues have been published online with *Grand Circle Travel*. The themes of travel, language, immigration, and justice are special for her.

Valerie Hunter teaches high school English and has an MFA in writing for children and young adults from Vermont College of Fine Arts. Her work has appeared in publications including *Room*, *Beneath Ceaseless Skies*, *The Quiet Reader*, and *Edison Literary Review*. You can find her on Instagram at @somanystories_solittletime.

Erin Jamieson holds an MFA in creative writing from Miami University of Ohio. Her writing has been published in over eighty literary magazines, and her fiction has been nominated for a Pushcart Prize. She teaches at Ohio State University.

Grace McGory is a queer artist and storyteller from New Jersey. She is working toward two bachelors of arts degrees in theatre and writing arts at Rowan University. Grace is the proud winner of a New Jersey Governor's Award in Arts Education, a Denise Gess Literary Award in short fiction, and the Kean Stages Senior Endeavor Award. When she's not writing, Grace enjoys baking, embroidery, and telling anyone who will listen about how cool ravens are.

Veronica Nation (she/her/hers) is a Colorado poet and artist whose work has been featured in *Capsule Stories*, *The Allegheny Review*, *300 Days of Sun*, and other literary journals. In her spare time, Veronica enjoys drinking iced coffee, immersing herself in yellow, and taking pictures of things she loves. You can read her writing on her website at veronicanation.com and on Instagram at @rainandpoetry.

Esther Lim Palmer is the author of two chapbooks, *Stellar* (Finishing Line Press, 2021) and *Janus* (Finishing Line Press, 2020). Her work has appeared in various literary journals and anthologies, including *California Quarterly*, *Plainsongs*, *White Wall Review*, *Poetry in the Time of Coronavirus Volume 2*, *The Hungry Chimera*, *Brief Wilderness*, and *Oberon*'s Seventeenth Annual Issue—selected to be archived in the EBSCO Humanities' database for universities and cultural entities interested in contemporary literary work.

Baylee Pawsey is a writer from the Midwest who spends her days crafting marketing content for a global tech company. As a freelance writer and editor, she works with local authors, entrepreneurs, and professionals. Outside of work, Baylee enjoys escaping into novels and video games, and she's always looking for good recommendations of both! Follow her on Twitter at @BayleeWrites and check out her work at bayleewrites.com.

Tammy Pieterson is a twenty-six-year-old South African student, poet, artist, and photographer. Creativity is all she's good at. Enthusiastic, passionate, and opinionated, she uses each day to learn more about herself, and therefore, more about each of her crafts and how to better apply herself. She believes in authenticity and vulnerability when writing, as it helps to connect with the reader—with the soul. So far, her poetry has been published in *Blue Daisies*, *Sunday Mornings at the River*, *decurated*, *Color Tag Magazine*, *Eclipse Zine*, *Pile Press*, and *Querencia Press*, and her artwork has been published in *Talent Spark Magazine* and *Stuck in Notes*. She's grateful, eager, and only getting started.

William Reichard is a writer, editor, and educator. His seventh poetry collection, *Our Delicate Barricades Downed*, was published by Broadstone Books in 2021.

Erika Seshadri lives on an animal rescue ranch in Florida with her family. When not caring for tame critters or feral children, she can be found writing.

Lesley Sieger-Walls holds a PhD in English from the University of Illinois. A Kansas native, she now lives in St. Louis, Missouri, where she teaches college writing classes and conducts walking tours for the Missouri Historical Society. Her poetic focus is typically rooted in the landscapes of the Great Plains and Midwest.

Kat Smith (@material.drifter) is a queer multimedia artist drawn to fibers, printing, and writing, often times melding these mediums together. Their work drifts toward natural and mystic worlds with their process serving as a meditative act.

Russell Thorburn is the author of five books of poems, including *Somewhere We'll Leave the World* (Wayne State University Press, 2017) and his newest book, *Let It Be Told in a Single Breath* (Cornerstone Press, 2024). He has received numerous grants, including a National Endowment for the Arts Fellowship. His radio play, *Happy Birthday, James Joyce*, was aired on WNMU-FM three times, and his one-act play, *Gimme Shelter*, was scheduled to premiere at Northern Michigan University's Black Box Theatre on March 13, 2020, but was canceled because of the pandemic. Thorburn was nominated and chosen as the first poet laureate of the Upper Peninsula in 2013.

Lotte van der Krol is a Dutch writer who writes stories and poetry that range from fantasy to horror to everyday-but-not-quite-normal fiction. She likes to walk in the woods and swim in rivers, and then write about those things. Her work has been published by *Popshot Quarterly*, *Second Chance Lit*, *Small Leaf Press*, and others. Online you can find her at lottevanderkrol.wordpress.com and on Twitter at @lottevdkrol.

Danielle Weeks earned her MFA in poetry through Eastern Washington University's creative writing program. Her poetry has been published or is forthcoming in *Crab Creek Review*, *The Gettysburg Review*, *The Missouri Review*, and *Salt Hill*, among others. Read more about her and her work at daniellekayeweeks.com.

Izzy Amber Wyskiel is an autistic writer living in Oregon. She loves reading literary fiction novels and story collections, watching horror movies, and cooking plant-based food. Her work is inspired by the beauty in mundanity, quiet yet vivid memories, and the neurodivergent lens. Her work is forthcoming in *Apple a Day Volume 1* by Bitter Pill Press. You can find her on Instagram at @kriziaamber.

Michelle Yim (she/her) is a young Korean American writer. She plans to study English literature in college and has been published in young adult literary magazines. She enjoys art and wants to publish her own YA novel in the future.

Editorial Staff

Natasha Lioe, Founder

Natasha Lioe graduated with a BA in narrative studies from University of Southern California. She's always had an affinity for words and stories and emotions. Her work has appeared in *Adsum Literary Magazine*, and she won the Edward B. Moses Creative Writing Competition in 2016. Her greatest strength is finding and focusing the pathos in an otherwise cold world, and she hopes to help humans tell their unique, compelling stories.

Carolina VonKampen, Publisher and Editor in Chief

Carolina VonKampen graduated with a BA in English and history and completed the University of Chicago's editing certificate program. She is available for hire as a freelance copyeditor and book designer. For more information on her freelance work, visit carolinavonkampen.com. Her writing has appeared in *So to Speak*'s blog, *FIVE:2:ONE*'s #thesideshow, *Moonchild Magazine*, and *Déraciné Magazine*. Her short story "Logan Paul Is Dead" was nominated by *Dream Pop Journal* for the 2018 Best of the Net. She tweets about editing at @carolinamarie_v and talks about books she's reading on Instagram at @carolinamariereads.

Claire Taylor, Editor

Claire Taylor is a writer in Baltimore, Maryland, where she lives with her husband, son, a bossy old cat, and an anxious dog who longs to be the cat's best friend. Claire's writing has appeared in a variety of publications, and she was a finalist for the 2020 Lascaux Prize in Poetry and winner of the 2021 *Serotonin* New Year's Day poetry competition. Her micro-chapbook, *A History of Rats*, is available from Ghost City Press. Claire is the founder and editor in chief of *Little Thoughts Press*, a print literary magazine of writing for and by kids. Claire

---

joined *Capsule Stories* as a reader in March 2021. A selection of Claire's work is available online at clairemtaylor.com.

BEE LB, Reader

BEE LB is an array of letters, bound to impulse; they are a writer creating delicate connections. they have called any number of places home; currently, a single yellow wall in Michigan. they are currently working on two poetry manuscripts, *HEART GROTESQUE* and *SWALLOW THE TRUTH, COUGH UP BOTH HALVES*. they have been published in *Revolute Lit*, *Red Weather*, *opia*, *Capsule Stories*, *Catchwater Magazine*, and *Ample Remains*, among others. they joined *Capsule Stories* as a reader in January 2022. their portfolio can be found at twinbrights.carrd.co.

Aimee Brooks, Reader

Aimee Brooks (she/her) is a writer from West Texas making her way in the Pacific Northwest. She is attending Eastern Washington's MFA program to hone her skills and immerse herself in a community of writers. When she's not sitting at her desk, cup of coffee in hand, she's exploring trails with her husband, picking berries, and trying to train her cat to walk on a leash. You can find more of Aimee's work in *Goats Milk Magazine*, *Embers* literary magazine, and The Storytelling Project. Follow her bookstagram at @bookie.of.the.year.

Stephanie Coley, Reader

Stephanie Coley is a country girl from Gering, Nebraska. She graduated in 2016 from Concordia University, Nebraska with a BA in English and a minor in art. She has been a journalism teacher, janitor, data technician, and more. Stephanie is a published poet, appearing in the National Creativity Series of 2009 and *Mango* Issue 3, Respeto, in 2017. She is also a winner of the 2020 Historic Posters Reimagined Project, which can be found at the Nebraska History Museum in Lincoln, Nebraska. Stephanie currently works as the program manager at the West Nebraska Arts Center in Scottsbluff, Nebraska. Stephanie joined *Capsule Stories* as a reader in January 2021.

Rhea Dhanbhoora, Reader

Rhea Dhanbhoora worked for close to a decade as an editor and writer before quitting her job and moving to New York to get her master's degree and finally writing the stories everyone told her no one would ever read. Her debut poetry collection, *Sandalwood-Scented Skeletons*, was published by Finishing Line Press in 2022. Her work has appeared or is forthcoming in publications such as *Sparkle & Blink, Awakened Voices, Five on the Fifth, Capsule Stories Autumn 2020 Edition, Fly on the Wall Press, HerStry, Artsy, Broccoli Mag,* and *JMWW.* Her work has been nominated for a Pushcart Prize and Best American Essays. She is currently on the board of directors for the literary organization Quiet Lightning and editor of RealBrownTalk. Rhea joined *Capsule Stories* as a reader in January 2021. She's working on several projects, including a linked story collection about women based in the underrepresented Parsi Zoroastrian diaspora. You can read her work online at rheadhanbhoora.com.

Hannah Fortna, Reader

Hannah Fortna graduated in 2016 from Concordia University, Nebraska, combining her passion for the written word and her affinity for art making with a degree in English and a minor in photography. After a three-year career as a freelance copyeditor, she heard traveling calling her name and now works seasonal jobs in places connected to America's national parks. When she's not selling souvenirs to tourists in gift shops, she enjoys hiking, photographing natural spaces, and writing about the flora and fauna she saw while on the trail. She reads anything from poetry to middle-grade novels, but the nature-inspired creative nonfiction section is her haunt in any bookstore. Her poetry has previously appeared in *Moonchild Magazine* and *Capsule Stories Spring 2019 Edition*. Hannah joined *Capsule Stories* as a reader in November 2020.

Teya Hollier, Reader

Teya Hollier is a graduate of York University with a BA in creative writing. At York, she won both the Babs Burggraf Award and the Judith Eve Gewurtz award for her poetry and prose. Her work has previously appeared in *Room* magazine, *Verses Magazine*, *OyeDrum Magazine*, and *Capsule Stories Second Isolation Edition*, where she was nominated for a Pushcart Prize. Teya joined *Capsule Stories* as a reader in January 2022. When she is not writing, she is reading and reviewing books, watching horror movies, drinking copious amounts of tea, and bingeing *The Great British Bake Off*. She is currently working on a collection of short stories and a ghostly novella.

Mel Lake, Reader

Mel (Melodie) Lake is a writer and editor who lives in Denver with her partner and a very good dog. She received an English BA from Northern Arizona University and an MS in technical communication from Northeastern University. Her essays have been published in *The Mark Literary Review* and *Capsule Stories* and her fiction in various places including *Stratum Press* and *Land beyond the World*. The full list of her publications can be found at mel-lake.com. She's working on a novel, is a comics nerd, and always forgets to tweet at @melofsometrades. Mel joined *Capsule Stories* as a reader in January 2022.

Kendra Nuttall, Reader

Kendra Nuttall is a copywriter by day and poet by night. She has a BA in English with an emphasis in creative writing from Utah Valley University. Her work has previously appeared in *Spectrum, Capsule Stories, Chiron Review,* and *What Rough Beast,* as well as various other journals and anthologies. She is the author of the poetry collection *A Statistical Study of Randomness* (Finishing Line Press, 2021) and *Our Bones Ache Together* (FlowerSong Press, forthcoming). Kendra lives in Utah with her husband and poodle. When she's not writing, you can find her hiking, watching reality TV, or attempting to pet every animal she sees. You can find out more about her work at kendranuttall.com. Kendra joined *Capsule Stories* as a reader in January 2021.

Rachel Skelton, Reader

Rachel Skelton graduated from William Woods University with a BA in English, a concentration in writing, and a secondary major in business administration, a concentration in management. She has interned for Dzanc Books and now works as a freelance fiction editor specializing in speculative fiction. You can find more information about her work at theeditingskeleton.com. She occasionally tweets about editing at @EditingSkeleton and talks about books she's reading at @TheReadingSkeleton on Instagram. When she's not doing anything reading-related, she's hanging out with her cats, collecting houseplants, and attempting to learn how to crochet. Rachel joined *Capsule Stories* as a reader in January 2021.

Deanne Sleet, Reader

Deanne Sleet is a graduate of Saint Louis University with a BA in English, a concentration in creative writing, and minors in African American studies and women's and gender studies. She has interned for *River Styx* and Midwest Artist Project Services, where she gained experience with grant writing, editing, and writing copy. She is currently the leasing and marketing manager at City Lofts on Laclede and holds the secretary position for SLU's Black Alumni Association. She writes short fiction and poetry, and a novel is in the making. In her spare time, she hangs out with her cat and roller-skates. Deanne joined *Capsule Stories* as a reader in February 2021.

Annie Powell Stone, Reader

Annie Powell Stone (she/her) is a fan of peanut butter toast. Her work has appeared in over a dozen print and online journals; she joined *Capsule Stories* as a reader in March 2022. Annie got her BA in English from the University of Maryland and her MS in education from the University of Pennsylvania. She lives on the ancestral land of the Piscataway people with her husband and two kiddos in Baltimore City, Maryland. Annie enjoys guerilla gardening and teaching kids to read. Read more of her poetry by following her on Instagram at @anniepowellstone.

Emily Uduwana, Reader

Emily Uduwana (she/her) is a poet and short fiction author based in California. She received her BA in history from CSU Northridge and her MA in history from UC Riverside, where she focused on queerness, gender, and sexuality in early California. Her work can be found on her website and in publications like *FUNGI Magazine*, *Stonecoast Review*, and *Capsule Sto-*

ries Autumn 2021 Edition. Her debut poetry chapbooks, *Knotted* and *An Expedition to the Desert of Andromeda*, were released in 2020 by orangeapplepress and Roaring Junior Press. Her next chapbook and first collection are forthcoming from Louisiana Literature Press and Nightingale & Sparrow Press in 2022. Emily joined *Capsule Stories* as a reader in January 2022.

Amy Wang, Reader

Amy Wang is a student from California. Her work has been recognized by the Scholastic Art and Writing Awards, the YoungArts Foundation, and Columbia College Chicago, among others. In her free time, you can find her crying over fanfiction or translating Chinese literature. Amy joined *Capsule Stories* as a reader in January 2022.

Submission Guidelines

Capsule Stories **is a print literary magazine** published once every season. Our first issue was published on March 1, 2019, and we accept submissions year-round.

Become published in a literary magazine run by like-minded people. We have a penchant for pretty words, an affinity to the melancholy, and an undeniably time-ful aura. We believe that stories exist in a specific moment, and that that moment is what makes those stories unique.

What we're really looking for are stories that can touch the heart. Stories that come from the heart. Stories about love, identity, the self, the world, the human condition. Stories that show what living in this world as the human you are is like.

We accept short stories, poems, and remarkably written essays. For short stories and essays, we're interested in pieces under 3,000 words. You may include up to five poems in a single poetry submission (please send them all in one Word document), and only send one story or essay at a time. Please send previously unpublished work only ("published" includes pieces that have been posted or made publicly available on a blog, website, or social media platform). You may only submit one submission per edition. Simultaneous submissions are okay, but please let us know if your submission is accepted elsewhere. Please include a brief third-person bio with your submission, and attach your submissions in a Word document (no PDFs unless your poetry has very specific formatting, please!).

Find our full submission guidelines and current theme descriptions at capsulestories.com/submissions.

Connect with us!
capsulestories.com
@CapsuleStories on Twitter and Facebook
@CapsuleStoriesMag on Instagram

CPSIA information can be obtained
at www.ICGtesting.com
Printed in the USA
BVHW012151090223
658258BV00018B/612